GW00891125

PLAYGROUND GAMES

with rhymes and chants

Julie Ashworth   John Clark

Illustrated by David Parkins

LONGMAN

CONTENTS

The chaser
(It)

INTRODUCTION

The games in this book are traditional English games. Some of the games have rhymes or chants. They are played in the playground or the street. You can play these games in any large space.

These games usually include running and chasing. The *chaser* is the person who runs after the other players. The *chaser* is sometimes called *it*.

Choosing the *chaser* is an important part of the game. Some rhymes for choosing are on pages 4 and 5.

Have fun!

← The players →

Choosing Rhymes

Many games have a *chaser*. You must choose the *chaser* before the game. You can use rhymes.

You say this rhyme only once.

> A-B-C-D-E-F-G-H-I-J-
> K-L-M-N-O-P-Q-R-S-T-
> you are it!

You say this rhyme more than once.

> One potato, two potato, three potato, four,
> Five potato, six potato, seven potato,
> MORE!

You say this rhyme more than once.

> Dip, dip, dip,
> My blue ship,
> Sailing on the water
> Like a cup and saucer.
> Dip, dip, dip,
> You're not it!

You say this rhyme more than once. The words have no meaning. They are for fun.

> Ibble, obble, black bobble,
> Ibble, obble, out!

BRITISH BULLDOG

← The bulldog

The players stand next to one wall.

One player is the *bulldog*. The *bulldog* stands in the middle.

The *bulldog* shouts, **'Go'**. The players run to the other wall.
The *bulldog* tries to touch someone.

GO!

If she touches someone, they are a *bulldog* too.

Then the players run back to the first wall.

Play the game until all the players are *bulldogs*.

GO!

Two
bulldogs →

6

POISON

The *chaser* holds out his hands.

Each player holds a finger.

The *chaser* says,
'I went to the shop and I bought a bottle of . . .' (anything in a bottle e.g. lemonade, cola, orange juice, vinegar).

If the *chaser* says **'Poison'**, the players run. The *chaser* tries to touch them.

If she touches someone, they are *it*.

> I went to the shop and I bought a bottle of p-p-p-pepsi!

The chaser

> I went to the shop and I bought a bottle of POISON!

7

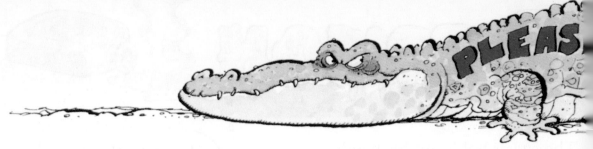

The players stand behind one line.

One player is *Mr Crocodile*.
Mr Crocodile stands in the middle. He is in the 'river'.

The players shout,
'Please, Mr Crocodile, can we cross your river?'

Mr Crocodile answers,
'No, you can't. Unless you're wearing . . .'
(he picks a colour e.g. red).

The players wearing (red) walk across the river.
Mr Crocodile can't touch them.

The players not wearing (red) run across the river.
Mr Crocodile tries to touch them.

If *Mr Crocodile* touches someone, they are a *crocodile* too.

Play the game until all the players are *crocodiles*.

MR. CROCODILE!

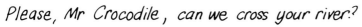

Please, Mr Crocodile, can we cross your river?

No, you can't! Unless you're wearing blue.

← Two crocodiles

What's the Time, Mr Wolf?

One player is *Mr Wolf*. *Mr Wolf* walks slowly.

The players walk slowly towards *Mr Wolf* and shout,
'What's the time, Mr Wolf?'
Mr Wolf turns around quickly and shouts,
'One o'clock'.

Mr Wolf turns around and walks again.
The players get nearer and nearer to *Mr Wolf*.
They ask, **'What's the time, Mr Wolf?'** again.

If *Mr Wolf* shouts **'Dinner time!',** he runs after the players.
He tries to touch one of them.

If he touches someone, they are *Mr Wolf*. The game starts again.

FROG IN THE MIDDLE

One player is the *frog*. The *frog* sits on the floor. He can't stand up.

The players stand in a circle around the *frog*.
They touch him and prod him. They shout,
'Frog in the middle, you can't catch me'.

The *frog* tries to touch someone.

If he touches someone, they are the *frog*.

Lucy

This game needs twelve players or more.

The players sit in a big circle. One player is *Lucy Locket*. *Lucy Locket* stands outside the circle. She has a handkerchief.

Lucy Locket walks slowly around the circle. The players sing,
'Lucy Locket lost her pocket,
Where did she drop it?
Drop it. Drop it . . .'

Locket

Lucy Locket drops the handkerchief and starts to run. The players stop singing.

The player nearest to the handkerchief picks it up quickly. He runs around the circle in the opposite direction.

The first player to run around the circle and sit down is the winner. The loser is now Lucy Locket.

13

QUEENIE

One player is *Queenie*.

Queenie has a small ball. She throws the ball over her head.
One player picks up the ball. She hides it behind her back.
Then the players stand in a line.

Queenie

The players shout,
'Queenie, Queenie who's got the ball?
Is she big or is she small?
Is she fat or is she thin?
Or is she like a rolling pin?

Queenie turns around. She guesses who has got the ball.
If she is right, she is *Queenie* again. If she is wrong, the player
with the ball is *Queenie*.

Queenie, Queenie, who's got the ball?
Is she big or is she small?
Is she fat or is she thin?
Or is she like a rolling pin?

(N.B. = a rolling pin.)

14

TIG

One player is the *chaser*.

The *chaser* runs after the other players. She tries to touch them.

If she touches a player she shouts **'Tig!'**. The game starts again with the new *chaser*.

TIG!
You're it!

CHAIN TIG

One player is the *chaser*.

The *chaser* runs after the other players. He tries to touch them.

If he touches a player he shouts **'Tig!'**. These two players hold hands. They try to touch the other players.

15

GAMES FOR TWO

Stand back to back.
Bend down and hold hands.

Try to pull the other player
to your line.

Sit on the floor. Put your feet together. Hold hands.

Shout, **'One – two – three – pull!'**.
Try to lift the other player off the ground.

GW00891132

Wee Willie Winkie
& other
Nursery Rhymes

Bright ☆ Sparks

This is a Bright Sparks Book
First published in 2000
Bright Sparks
Queen Street House
4 Queen Street
Bath BA1 1HE, UK

Copyright © Parragon 2000

This book was created by
The Albion Press Ltd
Spring Hill, Idbury,
Oxfordshire, OX7 6RU, UK

Cover design by
small world creations ltd
Tetbury, GL8 8AA, UK

Printed in China

All rights reserved

ISBN 1-84250-123-2

Contents

TWO LITTLE DICKY BIRDS

Two little dicky birds sitting on a wall,
One named Peter, one named Paul.
  Fly away, Peter!
  Fly away, Paul!
    Come back, Peter!
    Come back, Paul!

THERE WERE TWO BIRDS SAT ON A STONE

There were two birds sat on a stone,
　Fa, la, la, la, lal, de;
One flew away, then there was one,
　Fa, la, la, la, lal, de;
The other flew after, and then there
　　was none,
　Fa, la, la, la, lal, de;
And so the poor stone was left all alone,
　Fa, la, la, la, lal, de!

LITTLE SALLY WATERS

Little Sally Waters,
Sitting in the sun,
Crying and weeping,
For a young man.
Rise, Sally, rise,
Dry your weeping eyes,
Fly to the east,
Fly to the west,
Fly to the one you love the best.

MR. NOBODY

Mr. Nobody is a nice young man,
He comes to the door with his hat in his hand.
Down she comes, all dressed in silk,
A rose in her bosom, as white as milk.
She takes off her gloves, she shows me her ring,
Tomorrow, tomorrow, the wedding begins.

OLIVER TWIST

Oliver Twist
You can't do this,
So what's the use
Of trying?
Touch your toe,
Touch your knee,
Clap your hands,
Away we go.

A SAILOR WENT TO SEA

A sailor went to sea, sea, sea,
To see what he could see, see, see,
But all that he could see, see, see,
Was the bottom of the deep blue sea, sea, sea.

I LOVE SIXPENCE

I love sixpence, pretty little sixpence,
  I love sixpence better than my life;
I spent a penny of it, I spent another,
  And took fourpence home to my wife.

Oh, my little fourpence, pretty little fourpence,
  I love fourpence better than my life;
I spent a penny of it, I spent another,
  And I took twopence home to my wife.

Oh, my little twopence, my pretty little twopence,
   I love twopence better than my life;
I spent a penny of it, I spent another,
   And I took nothing home to my wife.

Oh, my little nothing, my pretty little nothing,
   What will nothing buy for my wife?
I have nothing, I spend nothing,
   I love nothing better than my wife.

LITTLE BO-PEEP

Little Bo-peep has lost her sheep,
  And can't tell where to find them;
Leave them alone, and they'll come home,
  And bring their tails behind them.

Little Bo-peep fell fast asleep,
  And dreamt she heard them bleating;
But when she awoke, she found it a joke,
  For they were still a-fleeting.

Then up she took her little crook,
   Determined for to find them;
She found them indeed, but it made her
      heart bleed,
   For they'd left all their tails behind'em.

It happened one day, as Bo-peep did stray
   Under a meadow hard by:
There she espied their tails side by side,
   All hung on a tree to dry.

IF ALL THE WORLD WAS
APPLE-PIE

If all the world was apple-pie,
   And all the sea was ink,
And all the trees were bread and cheese,
   What should we have for drink?

OLD BETTY BLUE

Old Betty Blue
  Lost a holiday shoe,
What can old Betty do?
  Give her another
  To match the other,
And then she may swagger in two.

HANDY SPANDY, JACK-A-DANDY

Handy Spandy, Jack-a-dandy
Loved plum-cake and sugar-candy;
He bought some at a grocer's shop,
And out he came, hop, hop, hop.

YANKEE DOODLE

Yankee Doodle went to town,
Riding on a pony;
He stuck a feather in his hat,
And called it macaroni.
   Yankee Doodle fa, so, la,
   Yankee Doodle dandy,
   Yankee Doodle fa, so, la,
   Buttermilk and brandy.

Yankee Doodle went to town
To buy a pair of trousers,
He swore he could not see the town
For so many houses.
   Yankee Doodle fa, so, la,
   Yankee Doodle dandy,
   Yankee Doodle fa, so, la,
   Buttermilk and brandy.

WASH, HANDS, WASH

Wash, hands, wash,
   Daddy's gone to plough;
If you want your hands washed,
   Have them washed now.

CLAP HANDS

Clap hands for Daddy coming
Down the wagon way,
With a pocketful of money
And a cartload of hay.

ADAM AND EVE AND PINCHME

Adam and Eve and Pinchme
Went down to the river to bathe.
Adam and Eve were drowned—
Who do you think was saved?

ME, MYSELF, AND I

Me, myself, and I—
We went to the kitchen and ate a pie.
Then my mother she came in
And chased us out with a rolling pin.

PETER PIPER

Peter Piper picked a peck of pickled pepper;
A peck of pickled pepper Peter Piper picked;
If Peter Piper picked a peck of pickled pepper,
Where's the peck of pickled pepper Peter Piper picked?

THE SHORTEST TONGUE-TWISTER

Peggy Babcock

OLD JOE BROWN

Old Joe Brown, he had a wife,
　She was all of eight feet tall.
She slept with her head in the kitchen,
　And her feet stuck out in the hall.

22

JEREMIAH

Jeremiah
Jumped in the fire.
Fire was so hot
He jumped in the pot.
Pot was so little
He jumped in the kettle.
Kettle was so black
He jumped in the crack.
Crack was so high
He jumped in the sky.
Sky was so blue
He jumped in a canoe.
Canoe was so deep
He jumped in the creek.
Creek was so shallow
He jumped in the tallow.
Tallow was so soft
He jumped in the loft.
Loft was so rotten
He jumped in the cotton.
Cotton was so white
He jumped all night.

THE GRAND OLD DUKE
OF YORK

The grand old Duke of York,
   He had ten thousand men;
He marched them up to the top of the hill,
   And he marched them down again!
And when they were up they were up,
   And when they were down they were down;
And when they were only halfway up,
   They were neither up nor down.

ANNA MARIA

Anna Maria she sat on the fire;

The fire was too hot, she sat on the pot;

The pot was too round, she sat on the ground;

The ground was too flat, she sat on the cat;

The cat ran away with Maria on her back.

HICKORY, DICKORY, DOCK

Hickory, dickory, dock,
The mouse ran up the clock.
The clock struck one,
The mouse ran down,
Hickory, dickory, dock.

THERE WAS A MAN AND HIS NAME WAS DOB .

There was a man, and his name was Dob,
And he had a wife, and her name was Mob,
And he had a dog, and he called it Cob,
And she had a cat, called Chitterabob.
  Cob, says Dob,
  Chitterabob, says Mob,
  Cob was Dob's dog,
  Chitterabob Mob's cat.

WE'RE ALL IN THE DUMPS

We're all in the dumps,
For diamonds and trumps,
The kittens are gone to St. Paul's,
The babies are bit,
The moon's in a fit,
And the houses are built without walls.

RING-A-RING O' ROSES

Ring-a ring o' roses
A pocket full of posies,
A-tishoo! A-tishoo!
We all fall down.

HIGGLETY, PIGGLETY, POP!

Higglety, pigglety, pop!
The dog has eaten the mop;
The pig's in a hurry,
The cat's in a flurry,
Higglety, pigglety, pop!

FOR EVERY EVIL UNDER THE SUN

For every evil under the sun,
There is a remedy, or there is none.
If there be one, try and find it;
If there be none, never mind it.

SALLY GO ROUND THE MOON

Sally go round the moon,
Sally go round the stars;
Sally go round the moon
On a Sunday afternoon.

WEE WILLIE WINKIE

Wee Willie Winkie runs through the town,
Up-stairs and down-stairs in his nightgown,
Peeping through the keyhole, crying through the lock,
"Are the children in their beds, it's past eight o'clock?"

STAR LIGHT, STAR BRIGHT

Star light, star bright,
First star I see tonight,
I wish I may, I wish I might,
Have the wish I wish tonight.